J 629.224 How
Howell, Brian
Monster trucks : tearing it up
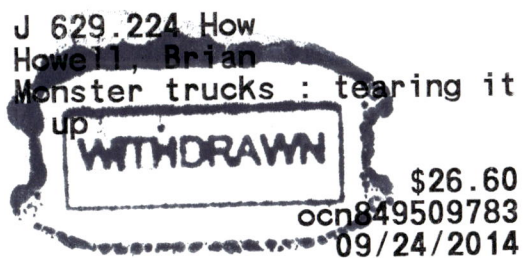
$26.60
ocn849509783
09/24/2014

MONSTER TRUCKS
TEARING IT UP

BY BRIAN HOWELL

Ŀ Lerner Publications Company • Minneapolis

Copyright © 2014 by Lerner Publishing Group, Inc.

All rights reserved. International copyright secured. No part of this book may be reproduced, stored in a retrieval system, or transmitted in any form or by any means—electronic, mechanical, photocopying, recording, or otherwise—without the prior written permission of Lerner Publishing Group, Inc., except for the inclusion of brief quotations in an acknowledged review.

Lerner Publications Company
A division of Lerner Publishing Group, Inc.
241 First Avenue North
Minneapolis, MN 55401 U.S.A.

For reading levels and more information, look up this title at www.lernerbooks.com.

Content Consultant: Charlene Bower, Bower Motorsports Media

Main body text set in Folio Std Light 11/17.
Typeface provided by Adobe Systems.

Photo credits: The images in this book are used with the permission of: © ZUMA Press, Inc./Alamy, p. 5; © Andrzej Gorzkowski Photography/Alamy, p. 6; © Malcolm Clarke/AP Images, p. 7; © Bettmann/Corbis/AP Images, pp. 8-9; © Natursports/Shutterstock Images, pp. 10, 13, 14-15, 16-17, 20-21, 26, 28; © Paul Warner/AP Images, p. 10-11; © Robert E. Klein/AP Images, pp. 14, 19; © Charles Slate/The Sun News/AP Images, pp. 22-23; © Cal Sport Media/AP Images, p. 23; © Piotr Zajac/Shutterstock Images, p. 25; © Dave Wallis/Fargo Forum Newspaper/AP Images, pp. 26-27; © Kelly Jordan/The Florida Times-Union/AP Images, p. 29

Front cover: © Michael Stokes/Shutterstock.com (main); © Janis Smits/Shutterstock.com (background).

Library of Congress Cataloging-in-Publication Data
Howell, Brian, 1974–
   Monster trucks : tearing it up / by Brian Howell.
      pages   cm. — (Dirt and destruction sports zone)
   Includes index.
   ISBN 978–1–4677–2120–2 (lib. bdg. : alk. paper)
   ISBN 978–1–4677–2451–7 (e-Book)
   1. Monster trucks. I. Title.
TL230.5.M58H68 2014
629.224—dc23   2013020696

Manufactured in the United States of America
1 – VI – 12/31/13

TABLE OF CONTENTS

CHAPTER ONE
HISTORY OF MONSTER TRUCK RACING 4

CHAPTER TWO
MONSTER TRUCK MANIA 12

CHAPTER THREE
THE TRUCKS 18

CHAPTER FOUR
THE DRIVERS 24

Glossary 30
For More Information 31
Index 32
About the Author 32

CHAPTER ONE
HISTORY OF MONSTER TRUCK RACING

Adam Anderson slammed his foot on the gas pedal. His truck engine roared as he entered the arena. Anderson hit high speeds in his monster truck, Grave Digger the Legend. The sold-out crowd at Sam Boyd Stadium in Las Vegas, Nevada, on March 23, 2013, let out a loud cheer. Marc McDonald also sped through the arena in the truck El Toro Loco. The fans were making lots of noise.

The two trucks roared down the arena's dirt track during the final race of the Monster Jam World Finals. This is the biggest and final monster truck event each year. The trucks tour the United States with Monster Jam during the year. There are two types of monster truck contests. One is side-by-side racing. The other event is a freestyle competition in which monster trucks perform tricks.

In monster truck racing, two trucks race to the other end of the arena. The trucks do a turn around an obstacle and race back to the finish line. During the last part of the race, the trucks go over a ramp that launches them into the air. After landing, the first truck to reach the finish line is the winner.

Marc McDonald and his truck, El Toro Loco, fly through the air in a side-by-side race.

The 2013 Monster Jam World Finals were the first time Grave Digger the Legend won a big prize.

Twenty-four trucks take part in the Monster Jam World Finals. One truck is knocked out of the competition in each heat. Grave Digger the Legend and El Toro Loco were the only trucks left on March 23. One would be crowned the world champion of monster truck racing.

Grave Digger the Legend took a slight lead as the trucks reached the turning point at the opposite end of the arena. Anderson made a smooth turn, but so did McDonald. Then both trucks sailed through the air after they hit the jump. Anderson's truck kept the lead all the way to the finish line. Grave Digger the Legend earned its first big prize in monster truck racing.

The race lasted less than 20 seconds, but it thrilled the crowd. Monster trucks have been thrilling fans for more than 30 years.

Bigfoot's Beginning

Bob Chandler was living near Saint Louis, Missouri, in the 1970s. He owned a Ford F-250 pickup truck. He had trouble finding parts for his truck, so he opened a four-wheel-drive parts shop in 1975. This gave Chandler easier access to the parts he needed to fix up his truck.

WHY MONSTER?

It is believed the term *monster truck* was first used in the 1970s when Bob Chandler had 48-inch (122-centimeter) tires on his truck, Bigfoot. This made Chandler's truck taller than other competing trucks. Bob George, one of the owners of Truck-a-rama, a motorsports company, called Bigfoot a monster truck. The name stuck and has been used ever since.

Over time, Chandler made his blue pickup truck bigger and more powerful. He gave it 48-inch tires and a larger engine. He spent his weekends testing the limits of his vehicle with off-roading trips. Chandler was known for having a heavy foot on the gas pedal. He liked to drive fast. This earned him the nickname Bigfoot. Chandler painted the name Bigfoot on his truck.

Bob Chandler had no idea his truck Bigfoot would start a new sport in the United States and around the world.

Soon people began calling the truck Bigfoot. Because Bigfoot's size and power were so unique, four-wheel-drive truck fans in the Midwest took notice. Word spread about the huge truck. Chandler brought Bigfoot to a car show in Denver, Colorado, in 1979. It was the first time he was paid money to bring Bigfoot to an event, but it was not the last.

Chandler and Bigfoot began appearing at tractor pulls around the country. A tractor pull is a popular event in which drivers of powerful tractors compete to see who can pull a very heavy sled the farthest. Bigfoot gained more fame and appeared at even more events.

Bigfoot was featured in a 1981 movie called *Take This Job and Shove It*. The main character drove Bigfoot as his truck.

That was also the first year Chandler used his truck to crush cars. Chandler and Bigfoot crushed two junk cars by driving over them in a Missouri cornfield. Chandler was surprised at how easy it was for Bigfoot to crush a car.

Not long after, an event promoter asked Chandler to crush cars in front of a crowd. Bigfoot performed at a small show in Missouri. Then Chandler brought a second truck he named Bigfoot #2 to a show at the Silverdome in Pontiac, Michigan. It was Chandler's first time performing in front of a huge crowd. "They had 68,000 people show up," Chandler said. "I drove up on the cars, stopped, and waved to the crowd. Flash bulbs were going off and 30,000 people came over the walls."

Chandler and Bigfoot traveled around the United States in the early 1980s crushing cars and performing for fans.

Maximum Destruction and driver Tom Meents have become monster truck fan favorites.

Monster Truck Mania

The monster truck craze was under way. Chandler started it with Bigfoot, and others soon followed. Trucks with names such as Maximum Destruction, Snake Bite, and Carolina Crusher have become famous too.

Monster trucks have come a long way since Chandler's F-250 in 1975. Even Bigfoot has changed over the years. Chandler's desire for a bigger, badder truck started what has become a popular sport in the United States.

THE BIGGEST MONSTER

During the 1980s, monster truck owners around the nation tried to build the biggest monster trucks. Chandler decided to put an end to the competition. He built Bigfoot #5, which weighs 28,000 pounds (12,700 kilograms) and stands 15.5 feet (4.7 meters) tall. Chandler put 120-inch (304.8 cm) tires on Bigfoot #5—that is 10 feet (3 m)! This is nearly twice the size of the standard 66-inch (167.6 cm) tires used on most monster trucks. Bigfoot #5 is on display in Hazelwood, Missouri, at Bigfoot headquarters.

In the 1990s, Chandler retired from driving in competitions. But he still plays a big role in the sport, especially in its safety. Chandler cofounded the Monster Truck Racing Association. This group is focused on promoting safety in the monster truck industry.

Bigfoot #5 is the largest monster truck ever to have been built.

CHAPTER TWO
MONSTER TRUCK MANIA

When Chandler invented the monster truck in the 1970s, he had no idea what he was starting. Chandler simply wanted to see how big and powerful he could make his Ford pickup truck. Monster truck events have become family favorites around the country and the world nearly 40 years later. There are hundreds of monster truck events in the United States every year. More than 4 million people attend these events.

The sport is growing outside the United States as well. Monster Jam put together its first tour of Europe in 2004. The tour went through Belgium, Sweden, and Finland. More than 100,000 people attended those events. Monster truck organizations have also put on shows in Italy, the Czech Republic, and Costa Rica. With huge, powerful trucks doing tricks that other vehicles cannot, it is no wonder the sport has gained popularity in other parts of the world.

Most monster truck events include races and freestyle contests. The races put two monster trucks in an arena at the same time.

Monster Jam is a growing series around the world. Two drivers displayed their trucks and met with fans after a 2011 event in Barcelona, Spain.

When the green flag drops, the trucks roar down a straightaway. The trucks race to the other end of the stadium. The trucks make a tight turn before approaching a big jump. The big jump is over at least three or four cars. The first monster truck to cross the finish line wins. Most races last less than 20 seconds.

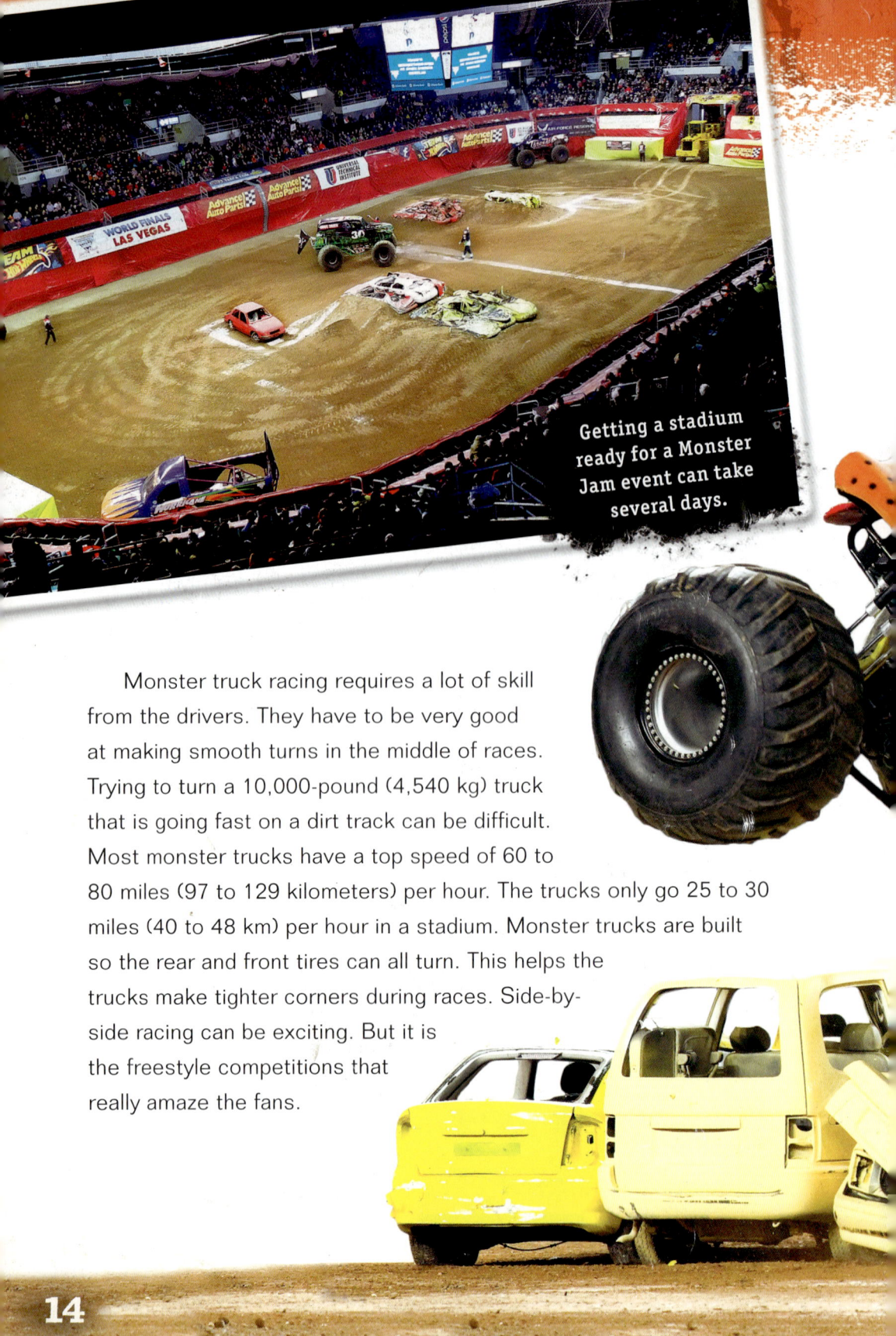

Getting a stadium ready for a Monster Jam event can take several days.

Monster truck racing requires a lot of skill from the drivers. They have to be very good at making smooth turns in the middle of races. Trying to turn a 10,000-pound (4,540 kg) truck that is going fast on a dirt track can be difficult. Most monster trucks have a top speed of 60 to 80 miles (97 to 129 kilometers) per hour. The trucks only go 25 to 30 miles (40 to 48 km) per hour in a stadium. Monster trucks are built so the rear and front tires can all turn. This helps the trucks make tighter corners during races. Side-by-side racing can be exciting. But it is the freestyle competitions that really amaze the fans.

CREATING THE TRACK

Many monster truck events are held in football stadiums. It takes a lot of work to convert a stadium's field into a monster truck track. Crews first lay down thousands of yards of plastic and thousands of sheets of plywood to protect the football field. Then, they fill the arena with dirt. Lots of dirt! More than 4,000 tons (3,630 metric tons) of dirt is used to create the track. Obstacles and junk cars are brought in as well. It can take crews from three to five days to get the arena ready for the monster trucks.

The freestyle competition is exciting to watch. Trucks such as the Mutt Rottweiler perform as many tricks as they can.

Sweet Tricks!

During freestyle competitions, one truck goes onto the track at a time. Each truck and driver has either 60 or 90 seconds to perform tricks. A driver is able to perform between four and six tricks during that time. Tricks can include spinning doughnuts, popping wheelies, jumping cars, crushing cars, and more. A doughnut is when a driver turns the truck in a tight circle, creating a doughnut shape in the dirt. At the Monster Jam World Finals, trucks must hit all the obstacles on the track and they must stay active throughout the time period.

Judges give scores to each truck on a scale of 1 to 10. The judges look for a variety of tricks. They also award points for high jumps, doughnuts, and other stunts. Drivers can lose points for backing up, stopping, or rolling over.

CRUSHED CARS

When Chandler crushed a pair of junk cars with Bigfoot in Pontiac, Michigan, in 1983, nearly 70,000 fans in attendance went crazy. Fans around the world have loved watching monster trucks crush cars ever since. More than 3,000 vehicles are crushed every year at Monster Jam performances. Those vehicles are typically borrowed from recycling centers and then returned after the show. The metal from the crushed cars is recycled.

One of the most amazing stunts occurred during the 2013 Monster Jam World Finals. Veteran driver Tom Meents performed a double backflip in his truck, Maximum Destruction. It was the first time a driver successfully landed the trick.

Trucks have jumped over airplanes, including a Boeing 727 jet. Longtime driver Dan Runte performed one of the greatest stunts while behind the wheel of Bigfoot #18. On September 16, 2012, in Indianapolis, Indiana, Bigfoot #18 set a new world record for the longest jump by a monster truck. The 10,000-pound vehicle raced off a ramp and flew an astonishing 214.7 feet (65.4 m) through the air. That is almost three-fourths the length of a football field.

Meents has landed some amazing tricks in his truck Maximum Destruction.

CHAPTER THREE

THE TRUCKS

A monster truck is a big pickup truck that weighs about 10,000 pounds. A regular pickup truck weighs between 3,000 and 4,000 pounds (1,362 and 1,816 kg).

Building a monster truck in the 1970s was simple. Chandler fixed up his Ford F-250 so it would support 48-inch (122 cm) tires. The tires were 50 percent bigger than those originally on the truck. Chandler then put 66-inch (168 cm) tires on Bigfoot #2. It was the first monster truck to feature such huge tires.

SAFETY FIRST

Because of the massive size and power of monster trucks, safety has become a main concern for drivers, crews, and race promoters. They all take great care to make sure fans and racers are safe. For example, remote ignition interrupters (RII) are installed in each truck. This cutoff switch allows an official to turn off the engine of a truck with a remote control. Officials use the RII when a truck crashes or appears to be out of control. Drivers wear fire suits and helmets with head and neck restraints. Drivers are very secure in their seats. This makes the impact of the jumps less stressful on the body and safer during a crash.

Most monster trucks have fun designs, such as the Monster Mutt truck.

Unique Truck Designs

After the tires, it is probably the body of the monster truck that fans notice first. Modern trucks are powerful, speedy pieces of art. Truck owners develop flashy paint jobs and designs that make each truck unique.

One of the best known modern trucks is Grave Digger. Dennis Anderson created this truck in the 1980s. Grave Digger has won several Monster Jam World Finals championships. The base colors of the truck are green and purple. The painted ghosts, haunted house, and tombstones make the truck stand out.

Monster Mutt is designed to look like a giant dog with actual ears that flip-flop as the truck jumps. Prowler looks like a big Bengal tiger. El Toro Loco is designed after a bull, with two large horns attached to the top of its roof. Many others have fun designs that draw attention in a crowded arena.

MAKING A MONSTER TRUCK

DESIGN
After it has been molded, the body of the truck gets a detailed paint job. A paint job can take 40 hours to complete. Most monster trucks are sponsored. These sponsors are featured on the trucks too.

TIRES
Most monster trucks have 66-inch (168 cm) wheels. This makes the trucks bigger. The average monster truck will go through eight tires per year.

DOORS AND HOOD

The doors and the hood of the truck don't open. This helps keep the driver safe if the truck crashes. Drivers crawl into the vehicle from underneath the truck or through the front windshield.

TRUCK BODY

The body of a modern monster truck is made of fiberglass. Fiberglass is a material made from plastic. This brings the total weight to around 150 pounds (68 kg) for the body of the truck. The fiberglass is molded to create a unique design for each truck. The fiberglass body covers a complete metal tube frame.

ENGINE

Monster trucks need a lot of power to crush cars and to launch into the air. Monster truck engines are five times more powerful than regular Ford F-150 pickup truck engines. A monster truck engine is designed for short, powerful bursts. Because so much power is needed, as many as 2.5 gallons (9.5 liters) of fuel are burned in a run of just a few hundred feet.

SUSPENSION SYSTEM

A suspension system connects the wheels to a truck. It also helps the truck absorb heavy impacts. Monster trucks are involved in a lot of jumps and crashes, leading to violent impacts with the ground. Modern trucks have suspension systems that protect the truck and the driver. Each tire has two shock absorbers. The shock absorbers are much longer than normal. This helps create a softer landing after a jump.

ON HIS FEET

Driver Frank Schettini designed one of the most unique monster trucks, named Monster Jerky. Schettini's truck has a stand-up driver's position. It is equipped with motorcycle-type shifters. His legs act as shock absorbers and help his body take impacts. Very few drivers have copied this setup, but it works for Schettini. "My advantage is more visibility," he said. "I have more control of the truck; everything is more second nature to me."

Monster trucks have changed over the years. One thing hasn't changed, though. Monster trucks are still capable of giving big crowds the thrill of a lifetime.

"Monster trucks have become more durable, and every driver has top-notch equipment," said Grave Digger creator Dennis Anderson, who has been driving monster trucks since the 1980s. "The biggest change for me, at least, is that the new generations of drivers are just running harder and harder and keep raising the bar, which ultimately makes Monster Jam so much better for the fans."

As the sport of monster trucks continues to grow, the experience becomes even better for fans.

Monster trucks and Monster Jam continue to grow their fan bases. Fans range in age, but many fans include families.

23

CHAPTER FOUR

THE DRIVERS

Getting behind the wheel of a 10,000-pound truck is a dream come true for many Monster Jam drivers. "I knew I wanted to be a monster truck driver at the early age of six after my mom took me to my very first show at the Pontiac Silverdome in 1986," said Bari Musawwir, who started driving in 2010. He drives the Spider-Man truck. Many of the elite drivers are just like Musawwir. They grew up loving racing, cars, and trucks. Most drivers started their racing careers in a different kind of vehicle.

GETTING STARTED

Some monster truck drivers get their start racing mud trucks or motorcycles. To get behind the wheel of a monster truck, a driver must obtain a commercial driver's license (CDL). A driver also must pass a driving test in a monster truck.

Even with a CDL and a successful driving test, many drivers spend years waiting for their chance to drive. A lot of drivers begin working for a monster truck team as a mechanic or an apprentice. Simply being

Many monster truck drivers grew up around racing and dreamed of driving a truck one day, including Bari Musawwir, who drives Spider-Man.

around a monster truck team is a good way for would-be drivers to get noticed. "I volunteered at shows whenever they were close to my area," said Cam McQueen, who won the 2012 Monster Jam Freestyle World Championship in his truck, Northern Nightmare. "Cleaning trucks, loading trailers, whatever they would let me do. My first driving opportunity came about when another driver was injured and I was asked to fill in."

FAMILY TRADITION

Dennis Anderson created one of the most famous trucks in history: Grave Digger. He has won multiple championships with Grave Digger. A legendary driver, he has passed the tradition on to his sons. Adam Anderson has won world championships while driving Taz and Grave Digger the Legend. Younger brother Ryan Anderson was the 2010 Monster Jam Rookie of the Year and drives Son-uva Digger.

25

Even though drivers compete against one another, many are great friends.

Just like other motorsports, a team supports the monster truck driver. A crew has at least three people. They make sure the truck is operational and fueled before each run. They also help make sure the truck moves safely out of an arena. To do this, the crew takes off the big tires, puts on smaller tires, and loads the monster truck onto a trailer after events. The crew takes the truck back to the shop to make any necessary repairs before the next event.

Love of Monster Trucks

While monster truck drivers come from many different backgrounds, they usually share two common bonds. They have a passion for the sport and a willingness to help one another.

"The thing that I found is the people that I go to the races with, if you're in dire need or trouble, they're over giving you a hand," said retired driver Steve Macklyn, who drove NitroFish. "The guy you may be racing in the next round is probably helping you out or maybe even loaning you parts, or vice versa."

The friendships among the drivers are part of what makes the sport so enjoyable for them. "I think that the most unique thing about monster trucks in general is the fact that we are all competitors on the track, but when we're off the track, we're all the best of friends," said Rick Swanson, owner and driver of two trucks, Obsession and Obsessed. "We will all do anything that we can for each other."

A monster truck crew is responsible for taking care of the truck and making sure it is ready for the next show.

MADUSA MAKES HISTORY

Debra Miceli, also known as Madusa, made Monster Jam history in 2004. Behind the wheel of her pink and white truck, Miceli became the first woman to win a Monster Jam championship. She won the freestyle competition that year. She was named racing champion in 2005. Madusa defeated the world famous Grave Digger in the finals. Through 2013 she was still the only woman to win a title.

Taryn Laskey is one of several women Monster Jam drivers. She competed in gymnastics and ballet as a young girl. And she started racing cars at the age of 10. Laskey made the jump to monster trucks in 2011 when she was 25. She passed her monster truck driving test that year and became a driver for the Monster Mutt Dalmatian team.

Miceli is the only woman to have won a Monster Jam title.

Before and after every event, monster truck drivers meet with fans. Fans can get drivers' autographs and see the trucks up close.

Monster Truck Fans

Perhaps the most unique aspect of monster truck racing is how the drivers and fans interact. Before every Monster Jam event, there is a pit party. Fans can go onto the racetrack and look at all the obstacles. They also get to meet the drivers.

"The drivers make themselves available for autographs and pictures before and after the event," Rick Swanson said. "We're there until the last fan leaves, signing T-shirts, signing pictures, whatever."

This interaction with fans is one of many reasons monster truck racing has become a popular form of family entertainment. But in the end, it is the desire to see monster trucks soar through the air and crush cars that brings fans to arenas year after year. For millions of fans around the world, watching massive machines doing amazing tricks is a thrill unmatched by anything else in motor sports.

GLOSSARY

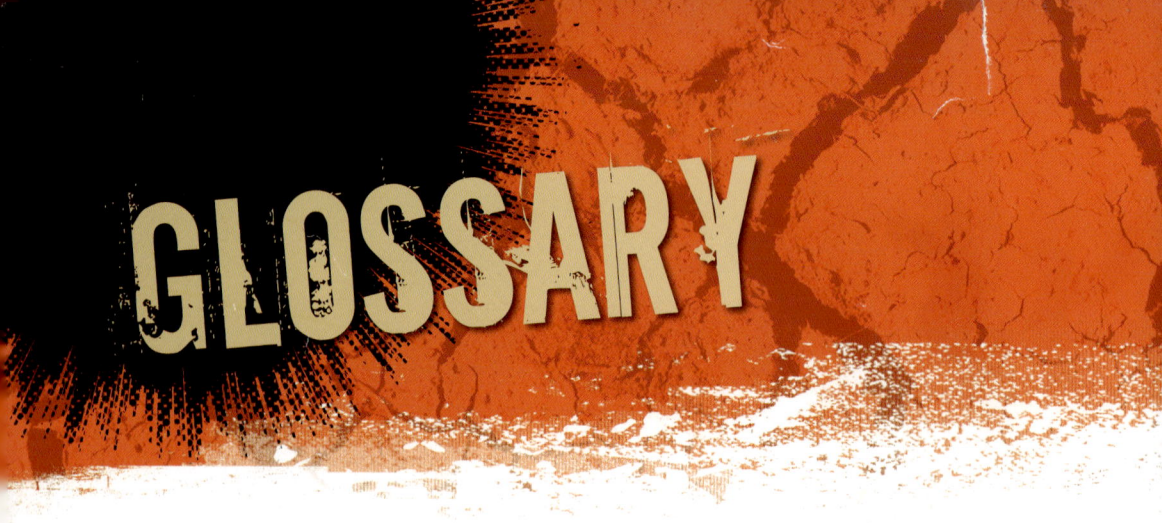

APPRENTICE
a person who works with someone else in order to learn a trade

BODY
the main part of a truck

DOUGHNUT
a truck spinning in a circle

EXHIBITION
a public event to show off skills or displays

FIBERGLASS
a lightweight material made from plastic

MECHANIC
a person who fixes cars

OBSTACLE
something that gets in the way

PROMOTER
a person financially responsible for a sporting event

SHOCK ABSORBERS
a device that absorbs energy from sudden movements of a vehicle

SUSPENSION
a system used to help trucks better absorb heavy impact and limit damage to the vehicle

FOR MORE INFORMATION

FURTHER READING

Gigliotti, Jim. *Monster Trucks.* Tarrytown, NY: Marshall Cavendish Benchmark, 2010.

Howell, Brian. *Mud Truck Racing: Tearing It Up.* Minneapolis: Lerner Publications Company, 2014.

WEBSITES

Bigfoot: The Original Monster Truck
http://www.bigfoot4x4.com/home.html
This is the website for the original monster truck: Bigfoot.

Grave Digger
http://www.gravedigger.com
The site features information and pictures for one of the most famous monster trucks in the world: Grave Digger.

Monster Jam
http://www.monsterjam.com
This is the official website for the biggest series in monster truck racing: Monster Jam.

INDEX

Anderson, Adam, 4, 6, 25
Anderson, Dennis, 19, 22, 25
Anderson, Ryan, 25

Bigfoot, 6–9, 10, 17
Bigfoot #2, 9, 18
Bigfoot #5, 11
Bigfoot #18, 17

Carolina Crusher, 10
Chandler, Bob, 6–9, 10–11, 12, 17, 18

doughnuts, 16

El Toro Loco, 4, 6, 19

Ford, 6, 12, 18, 21
freestyle competition, 4, 12, 14, 16, 28

George, Bob, 7
Grave Digger, 19, 22, 25, 28
Grave Digger the Legend, 4, 6, 25

Laskey, Taryn, 28

Macklyn, Steve, 26
Madusa, 28
Maximum Destruction, 10, 17
McDonald, Marc, 4, 6
McQueen, Cam, 25
Meents, Tom, 17
Miceli, Debra, 28
Monster Jam, 4, 12, 17, 22, 24, 25, 28–29
Monster Jam World Finals, 4, 6, 16–17, 19
Monster Jerky, 22
Monster Mutt, 19
Monster Mutt Dalmatian, 28
Monster Truck Racing Association, 11
Musawwir, Bari, 24

NitroFish, 26
Northern Nightmare, 25

Obsessed, 27
Obsession, 27

Pontiac Silverdome, 24
Prowler, 19

remote ignition interrupters, 18
Runte, Dan, 17

Sam Boyd Stadium, 4
Schettini, Frank, 22
side-by-side racing, 4
Snake Bite, 10
Son-uva Digger, 25
Swanson, Rick, 27, 29

Take This Job and Shove It, 8
Taz, 25
tractor pull, 8
Truck-a-rama, 7

wheelies, 16

ABOUT THE AUTHOR

Brian Howell is a freelance writer based in Denver, Colorado. He has been a sports journalist for nearly 20 years, writing about high school, college, and professional athletics. In addition, he has written books about sports and history. A native of Colorado, he lives with his wife and four children in his home state.

Harris County Public Library
Houston, Texas